Tips For Tricks

tips for tricks

An International Fun Guide

All you need to know to:

Be a Trick

Have a Trick

Want a Trick

Host a Trick

Or be hosted by one!

Tips for Tricks is a work of fiction. Names, characters, places, and incidents are either the product of the author's imagination or are used fictitiously. Any resemblance to actual persons, living or dead, events, or locales is entirely coincidental.

Copyright © 2009 by C. Edward Green, Agent

All rights reserved.

Published in the United States of America
by C. Edward Green, Agent, P.O. Box 14207
Cincinnati, OH 45250

ISBN: 978-0-9832950-0-6

Illustrations by	Book Design by
Glen Hanson; Toronto, Ontario	C. Edwards; Cincinnati, Ohio

Visit us at
www.tipsfortricksthebook.com

E-mail us at
edward@tipsfortricksthebook.com

All rights reserved. No part of this book may be reproduced, stored in a retrieval system, utilized, or transmitted in any form or by any means, electronic, mechanical, including photocopying, or otherwise without written permission of the publisher.

CONTENTS

GAYLY FORWARD

CHAPTER 1
    Online or On the Town
    — Do I really have to get dressed? 01

CHAPTER 2
    Dress for Success!
    — How to package the merchandise 05

CHAPTER 3
    Doing It Doggy Style
    — Truly a gay man's best friend 13

CHAPTER 4
    The Hunting Grounds
    — Maximizing the real estate 19

CHAPTER 5
    In the Sand
    — But not in your shorts or on the sheets 29

CHAPTER 6
    Hunting at the Bar
    — If you can't find a trick here we'll refund your TIPS purchase price 43

CHAPTER 7
    Ordering In
    — How to get a tasty mouthful and not from the chinese carryout 61

CHAPTER 8
    Your Place or Mine
    — Who launders the cum towels? 73

CHAPTER 9
    "No Glove, No Love" and Another Helpful Cliché
    — Two pithy points to remember 83

CHAPTER 10
    Top, Bottom and Upside Down
    — Is everyone REALLY a bottom? 89

CHAPTER 11
    Bailing Out
    — Just in case 95

CHAPTER 12
    The Main Event
    — Did someone say star power! 101

CHAPTER 13
    When to Come
    — Timing is everything! 107

CHAPTER 14
    When to Go
    — Breakfast is usually not included 113

CHAPTER 15
    After Action
    — Maximizing the moment 117

CHAPTER 16
    Into Fisting?
    — !!!!!!!!! 121

THE HAPPY ENDING 123

APPENDIX:
    Things You Want to Know; Ought to Know; Need to Know 127

AND... A REALLY COOL GLOSSARY 139

ACKNOWLEDGEMENTS

Not to brag, but way too many to remember.

(Tricks' names are overrated anyway)

GAYLY FORWARD

Webster's® defines **TOP**: "The **head** or top of the head, the choicest part, the **cream**, the pick. To gain ascendancy over, **to dominate**."

More Webster®: **BOTTOM** "A surface designed to support something resting on it, the **inmost point**, the **main plowing mechanism** of a plow. **Capacity**, as of a horse, **to endure strain**."

This whimsical little book is meant to expand your world, to give you ideas, strategies, and basic information on how to Trick.

Webster® gets us started but there is so much more to come.

You're horny. You feel that special throbbing in your crotch. It's a good urge, and hopefully soon to get even better. "It" grows at the office, on the street, at the gym. The other day, just standing at Starbucks, your pants could barely contain your bulge. You really need to get laid.

There is the option of your always reliable best-friend right-hand, but that's not what you want. You really want to Trick. You really need a Trick, a real live let's-get-naked-together Trick.

You have lots of choices, indeed some of them very choice choices: hunky or lean, top or bottom, passive or aggressive, younger or older, smooth or hairy. You know the kind of trick you want. And, like Halloween, that gay national holiday, Tricking and Treating go together.

This is a fun guide to help you navigate the tantalizing world of Tricking — where treats abound!

Enjoy!

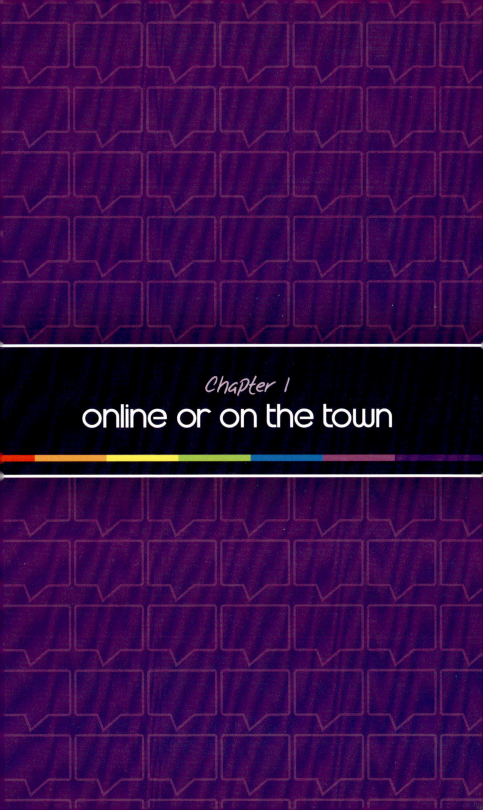

Chapter 1
online or on the town

Chapter 1

online or on the town
— *do I really want to get dressed?*

For the still cyber-challenged, there are the familiar and reliable on-the-town venues. Fortunately the tried and true, real life, seeing-is-believing bars and clubs, the drug stores and grocery aisles, the gym, the beaches, the parks, the shopping malls and your friends' cocktail parties or hot tubs still provide very fertile hunting grounds for Tricks!

Let's cover the in-person, seeing-is-believing, no screen-to-hide-behind hook-up first.

Don't worry, cyber tricking begins in Chapter 7, "Ordering In."

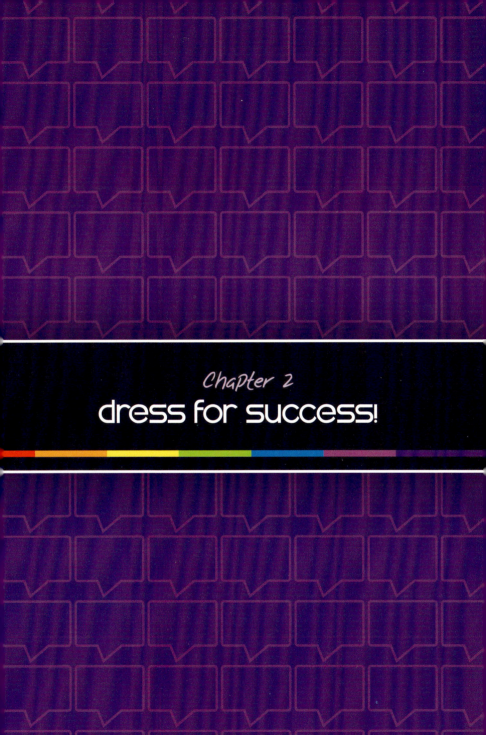

Chapter 2
dress for success!

Chapter 2

dress for success!
— how to package the merchandise

Dressing strategically is an art, an art mastered by gay guys.

You can adopt one of two "looks": the "put your best foot forward look" or slut wear. Both can be effective. Unfortunately beauty (or lust) is in the eye of the beholder so the end result isn't totally in your hands. But a good choice of age-appropriate (repeating, age appropriate!) threads can advance your cause!

If you look good in a polo shirt and khakis, then go for the preppy look. Nothing better than a well-fitting Polo to highlight

Chapter 2

those biceps and pecs! Note: "well fitted" means one size too small (although you probably knew that!)

Coat and tie can be a real turn on for some… maybe it's a fantasy that the form-firming starch in your collar will be matched by a form-firming something in your pants! Or maybe it's that tie conjuring up its own fantasies.

Shorts if you have good legs. Big boy pants for the rest.

Sandals work, flip flops don't. Flopping definitely sends the wrong message.

On the street, gym wear is a "two-fer." It's an outfit designed to show off your best assets and be a potential conversation starter, as well. "Where do you work out?" That likely is

Chapter 2

the most-asked question in gaydom. Your shorts, sneakers and tank top are guaranteed to start a conversation. Then it's just up to you to seal the deal where the "other" workout will take place. If you are an Adonis or a bear, a gym bunny or a big doughboy, gym wear can work for you. It shows what you've got and with gay tastes as varied as gym bags, there is someone out there for everyone.

The classic "come fuck me" look is the standard T shirt and jeans. Not baggy jeans but real, tight-fitting, ass-molding, pouch-showing jeans that show off your package and buns the way jeans were invented to do! (A big hard-felt thanks to Levi Strauss!) Some things are better not left to the imagination! And if you need a little help with your "presentation" a cell phone deep down in the front pocket is a good cheat!

Chapter 2

No pockets on the T's, but words can be a plus. The bicep-binding shirt becomes your "bait." They make it easy for someone to come up and start a conversation about your shirt's message... and you are half-way to the bedroom. Consider wearing shirts with small print across the chest. What it says isn't important... just gets him up close to "read" your chest. And hope for a slow reader who needs to use his finger to go word by word.

On your shirt, simple and subtle is way better than the in-your-face-way-too-cute-and obvious-gay-billboard shirt which is best read in windows of cheap and tacky clothing stores rather than worn in public. Trust us "Choking Hazard" is way overdone (and usually over-promised, as well!)

Now that you know how to dress, let's get you out in the world!

Chapter 3
doing it doggy style

Chapter 3

doing it doggy style
— truly a gay man's best friend

Before we explore the indoor hunting grounds, the absolutely, positively, all-time best "hook" you can use to attract a potential Trick is to walk a dog! Never fails. **Dogs are living man magnets.** No matter the breed, guys will stop and pet a dog, ask you about a dog, talk to a dog and eventually get around to talking to you... and that's the whole point. Dogs truly are a gay man's best friend. As a bonus, if you have some patience and your dog has any brains, train it to hump a guy's leg which gives you (or the humpee) the opening to say "Wow, he must take after his owner."

What image do you want to project with your dog – or the more important question, what impression will your potential Trick assume from your four-footed friend?

Chapter 3

If you are walking a Lab, be prepared to be approached by guys looking for a little friskiness, lots of energy, and sloppy tongue action!

A Boxer conjures up determination: Expect a very long, intense session! But who's watching the clock?

A Poodle or anything "fluffy" (even if you've named it Butch rather than Tiffany) marks you as a definite bottom with scented, 500-count Egyptian-cotton sheets on your bed.

If your Chihuahua gets lost in the high grass, trade up to a larger model!

A Doberman, the more intimidating the better, definitely projects an image of you as a Top.

Chapter 3

In contrast to the latest trend of "boutique" dogs like the Labradoodle and its ilk, the definite best of breed is the one with no breeding, the All-American mutt: no hang-ups, low maintenance, loves his tummy rubbed. Rolling over on his back is his idea of a good time! Gotta love 'em! What we all want in the four or two-legged playmates.

> *PS:* Looking for a way to earn some extra money? Here is some valuable financial advice from this valuable bookette. Set up a dog rental stand in any city park in the summer. Charge extra for horny dogs. Voila! See, this book has just paid for itself!

Chapter 4
the hunting grounds

Chapter 4

the hunting grounds
— *maximizing the real estate*

As in real estate, location, location, location. Here's our roadmap:

At the supermarket:

Never push a cart with two lamb chops, two sirloins or any other for-two foods. Better to be seen caressing the cucumbers or squeezing a couple of melons.

If you hook up, avoid becoming the cause of a loud-speaker announcement, "clean up in aisle four."

At the mall:

In general, Targé, not Walmart. BJ's Warehouse is a natural. Abercrombie and Fitch for younger. Brooks Brothers for older. But wherever, the place to hang is the place "they" hang.

Chapter 4

Try the men's jockey-short section. Fortunately with so many styles, you can linger quite a while!

At the drug store, the apothecary or the sex shop:

You can't go wrong dividing your time between lubes and condoms. But don't stand around holding a package of Magnums unless "the shoe fits" (and if so, wear it proudly!)

Speaking of lubes. Just reading the brands will give you an instant hard on: From the old standby KY® Jelly (now in a warming variety!) to the latest silicone-based products, there is something for everyone, from Liquid Silk® to Elbow Grease® with Wet®, Anal Eze®, Eros®, ID® Glide, Gun Oil®, Astroglide®, Boy Butter™, Manglide™ and Slick® in between! Instant fantasy land!

On the other hand, afraid of coming a bit too soon? Sta Hard®, Iron Man® and Stud 100® are available desensitizers that should do the Trick, literally!

Just remember: never an oil-based lube with latex condoms!

Chapter 4

On a cruise:

Whether it is Atlantis® or RSVP®, it's not called a "cruise" ship for nothing. The best things are the odds. You will be TRAPPED (nice ring to it?) aboard with several thousand gay guys looking for more than scenic wonders. And the odds are even better if you consider there also are a near-equal number of ship-trapped crewmen of various orientations. Never has "bondage" had so much potential.

First day on a cruise is an important one to get you started. Groups form quickly so assert yourself, add to conversations. When you spot a target, remember your trick of asking him questions - about him!

Be creative with your costumes for theme nights. Just as with swimwear, analyze your best assets and wear costumes that show them off. Don't wear a mask that hides your face or makes talking difficult.

Chapter 4

The Promenade Deck is aptly named or, just as ashore, cast your bait where you find the prey of your choice: the bars, the deck pools and hot tubs, the card rooms, the library, the gym. If your taste is universal, just hang out in your cabin with an open door! Extra points if the Captain comes calling.

And here is the key Tip: For those in the know or who want to be, the aft Deck 13 or 14 late at night is the place to be, clearly the best hunting ground while sailing under the rainbow flag.

At the gym:

Gym time is show-off time. Most gay guys are trying to make themselves attractive to others (and themselves!).

These fellows know that muscles, like dogs (see Chapter 3 on Doing It Doggy Style) make great bait for that potential Trick. Look around and snap up that bait.

Chapter 4

If you are into guys with hot legs, pecs, asses or abs, try to work out (thus hang out) among the machines designed to build those special body parts. That gives you a chance to observe (no drooling on the equipment, please) others building the parts you crave, to start a conversation, get acquainted, maybe exchange a cell number.

In the gym "opposites attract" is usually fallacious. Hard, built muscles usually do attract other hard, built muscles. But not always. Fantasies come in all sizes and shapes so whether you are a muscle stud or slightly-toned string bean, the gym has something for you.

Good gyms advise you to push your limits. That can be applied to making pick-up approaches as well. But be reasonable: remember you will be coming back day after day… to bulk up, to tighten up, to firm up, to chat up, and hopefully to pick up. That said, gyms provide the easiest pick-up lines anywhere.

Chapter 4

"Can you spot me?"

"Can I work in?"

"Mind if I work in?"

"Is anybody using this bench?"

"Great sixpack!"

"Who's your trainer?"

And of course… *"Where's the sauna?"*

Duh! Doesn't get any easier!

PS: Don't hang out among the 200-pound weights if you are a 120-pound weakling. Hernia's are not sexy.

Warning: Even if your gym has no limits for time spent in the steam room, your body does.

Chapter 5

in the sand
— but not in your shorts or the sheets

Whether your beach is Suma or Surfside, South Beach, Sebastian or Haulover, Black's Beach or the shores of Mykonos, FIP, Rehomo or Rio's Ipanema, some very helpful tricking advice:

As in any sport, (and cruising for a Trick is definitely a very-competitive activity) beach action requires the right equipment. (No pun intended! Sorta.)

The Towel

If you think the towel's only purpose is to dry off, you need a lesson in marketing. Take a big towel, one big enough to share: one big enough to encourage a drop-by to accept your invitation to sit down for a little conversation.

Chapter 5

In addition to serving (perhaps servicing is more appropriate) as hospitality mats, towels can be billboards, sharing your own sense of humor, carrying a message, acting as conversation starters.

Bottom line: Think BIG. That shouldn't be too hard, (oops, more Freud).

The Swim Suit

The shape of the swim suit you should be in depends much on the shape you are in. Pick out a swim suit that shows off your best features, minimizes your downers.
You spend a lot of time at the gym – and it shows. Work it! Tan those muscles up and watch them draw attention from the wannabees.

Too few gym hours in your recent history? Worry not. The old adage that there is someone out there for everyone applies to the beach as well as the bar.

Chapter 5

Legs and ass not your strong points? Loose-fitting surfer shorts will encourage lookers to zero in on one or more of your other assets, your eyes, your hair, your personality or drop-dead smile.

You have great buns, great legs? The Speedo was meant for you.

The new, designer built-in pouch swimsuits are engineering masterpieces and a boon for Trick-sters. Your package now always can be expertly packaged.

(But be forewarned: in P-Town, San Diego, or the Chicago Lake Shore, be seen near but not in those frigid waters. The physiology of cold water and asset shrinkage is undeniable... and undesirable... no matter how handsome the packaging.)

And yes, suit color does matter!

Chapter 5

Unless you are one of those lucky few who never fades, don't wear a white suit at the start of the season. Untanned skin against stark white trunks can look pasty. And if you get a little too much sun those first few days, your red skin will make you a thing to be pitied — a look to be avoided at all costs.

On the other hand, once your body has been bronzed to perfection, bright yellow or soft blue or white all work. Actually almost anything works against a deep tan.

However, as a generalization it is best to avoid suits in khaki or browns. Likewise for mauve or puce or any other color you can't identify by name. And leave the heavily-floraled to Hawaiians and those at the beach "with the Mrs."

> *PS:* A final word on white suits. If you are one of those who actually goes in the water, wear white only if you are willing to show off the family jewels... and they better be many carats!

Chapter 5

Beach Accessories

Remember you are not out in the searing sun for your health. You are here to get a Trick or be attractive to one even if you get your kicks out of turning down offers. The right accessories can help.

Liquid: An extra bottle or two of water is a no-brainer. Offering one on a hot day is an easy conversation starter.

Reading material: You don't like to read on the beach? Who cares. This is not for you, dummy. This is point-of-sale advertising when splayed out on your beach towel. As in fishing, the catch you seek determines the bait you use.

Into sophisticates? The arts section of the *Sunday NY Times* (or the latest issue of *Vanity Fair* if you are looking for those who like to dish.)

Into jocks? Any issue of *Sports Illustrated*, *Muscle & Fitness*, or any muscle magazine — certainly if you are on the cover!

Into professionals? Barrons, *The Wall Street Journal* or *GQ* or any magazine that has "Review" in the title.

Chapter 5

Into high brows? Any recent best-seller will get their attention.

Into a slightly lower brow? An issue of *Details*, *Out*, The latest tome on Judy Garland, the Merv Griffin book that trashes everyone in Hollywood or any book about the Oscars.

The local "gay rags" are also good, especially if you are looking for visitors, aka new meat. They always snatch them up. Offer to swap one for a phone number.

Or, if you honestly think there may be some question about your orientation, toss a recent issue of *The Advocate* on your rainbow-colored beach towel and remove all doubts.

Sporting Gear

If you can catch a football – you jock, you – a ball on your towel will get a game with the quarterback of your dreams.

Or display a Frisbee. Gentler, but still a great tool for finding someone to play with.

Paddleball is a hot sport on beaches, today. Two paddles on your towel invite a challenger.

Chapter 5

SPF

Some people think SPF stands for Suntan Protection Factor. And for some it does. But for those more in the know, there are other meanings and lessons to be learned about those who use it. SPF can mean **Sex Potential Factor**.

Before getting to the numbers, a "don't," a very important don't. Don't use lotion in aerosol spray cans. These terrible inventions negate one of the most important benefits from applying sun screen: the slow, sensuous, sensitive, sexy, prolonged massaging of the lotion into your skin in front of the whole envious beach, whether self-applied or with the aid of the talented and probing hands of your on-the-beach neighbor. Lustful and potentially-interested eyes watch that daily ritual from behind the latest designer sunglasses. And it is certainly appropriate to ask a friend (or stranger) to rub you in all those hard to reach places. The envy level skyrockets, not to mention a few observing crotches skyrocketing as well.

Chapter 5

There is a right way to have someone apply lotion to your back. Call it beach etiquette or beach opportunity. We recommend you bend half way over, placing both hands on your knees, i.e. assuming the position.

Now your face is appropriately at crotch level. If you prefer to give a different signal, of course, you can have him stand behind you. In either position, tell the Good Samaritan not to worry about getting lotion on your swim suit. In the interest of avoiding a burn line, (sure, right) you may want to encourage your new friend to run his fingers under the seams of the suit. You are foresighted if you see this as a lot like foreplay. You can safely take how far his fingers reach under your suit and the length of time he spends applying your lotion as indicators of his interest or lack of it.

Chapter 5

Good manners – as well as good opportunity – requires you to offer to reciprocate if someone applies your lotion. He will want you to use his lotion with its particular SPF rating and that serves your detective instincts because the SPF level of sun tan lotion is a solid giveaway into the bedroom practices of its user.

SPF 8: Carefree. Real Men. Hard Core. Can take as well as they give. Slap a little on and ready to go.

SPF 15: A bit more rational and more discerning. Studies the surrounding scenery. Good with eye contact (even behind those dark glasses) and a pro at positioning the pouch just so for maximum marketing effect. Nicely middle-of-the-road... probably versatile.

SPF 30: Likely accompanied by a book and a cooler with snacks and wine. Will spend a long time lotioning up which is a good indication of long foreplay to come. Fun to spend the day and/or night with.

Chapter 5

SPF 45: and higher: Often used on noses or tips of ears as a precaution against skin cancer. Users who bath their bodies in SPF 80 usually are found under an umbrella and never leave the safety of beach towel or blanket. Often with a friend for additional protection. As a generalization, way too cautious, way too much work and way too little fun.

PS: Although we discourage spray oils in general, if you do use them, use them strategically. Follow where the spray is actually going (which is likely not on your body on a windy day) and go up to the receiving Adonis where it landed and start up that apology-seeded conversation. Miss Manners would be so proud. And so would we.

Time to move indoors. But before we do, a final note on damage control. Alas, if, after contorting your arms like a spastic octopus in trying to get some lotion on the center of your back, some stranger does not offer to do the job for you, you are on infertile territory. Pick up your rainbow towel and relocate up the beach.

Chapter 6
hunting at the bar

Chapter 6

hunting at the bar
— if you can't find a trick here we'll refund your Tips purchase price

The odds of finding a Trick at a bar are great. However, there is both safety and danger in that hunting ground. Safety: one of your friends can warn you off if you are about to make a truly-tragic Trick choice. Danger: you might reject a good trick possibility simply because you fear a friend's personal negative judgment of your choice. Balance their "judgment" with their jealousies.

Straight Up or On the Rocks

Let's set some bar scenes, but first a word about alcohol.

Chapter 6

As we all know, too much alcohol before, no matter how you take it, straight up or on the rocks, martini glass or can of beer, can convert that nice firm rock hard into a meltdown. Assuming moderation, what can you tell about a potential Trick by what he drinks?

A quick (tongue in somebody's cheek) primer...

> **Beer:**
>
> **Domestic:** *down to earth, a jock or is convinced he is; "Bud complex"; sees himself as a "man's man"...and, come to think about it, what's wrong with that!*
>
> **Imported:** *An import drinker sees himself as a more worldly man's man; into the unusual... maybe kinky!*

Chapter 6

Scotch:

Sees himself as sophisticated and in control. Definitely a Top (at least in his own mind)

Dewar's®: Has a taster's tongue…..could prove interesting!

Famous Grouse's: The Queen's choice. 'Nuff said?

Glenfeddich®: If he can say Glenfeddich® properly when he orders, he has a very talented mouth!

Bourbon:

A Southern gentleman; wants to please; good bottom

The exception is "Jack on the rocks": has a nice ring to it and he's usually a top!!

Chapter 6

Gin:

Gin and Tonic: Summer is his favorite season. Also likes it hot in the bedroom with a tangy zest for exploring new positions! A good choice.

Dry Martini: Been around the world, also around the block; old hand at drinking.

Dirty Martini: Expect nasty talk in bed, the dirtier the better.

Rum and Coke®: Definite Latin influence; be prepared – extreme caution! expect an amazing and uncut experience.

"Cosmo": trendy, sometimes more show than go; think "Sex and the City"

Tequila: If there's a big worm, go for it!

Vodka:

Grey Goose®: Knows his booze; knows his preferences; "experienced"; and a long-necked goose creates a nice image.

Chapter 6

Ketel One® Martini: Sophisticate. May have a place at the Hamptons, or South Beach, or both!

Smirnoff®: Knows the name but a novice to alcohol (and the bedroom?)

Well Brand: These drinkers are cheap, easy and sleazy…. (gotta love those well drinkers)

Wine:

Whites are bottoms; **Reds** are tops. Just works that way.

Champagne drinkers? Very versatile… maybe it's the bubbles.

The non drinker:

If he asks for "no ice" in his "plain Coke®," don't expect great creativity in the bedroom. The upside: his tulip won't wilt from too much alcohol.

And the 2-1 Happy Hour? One can only hope it refers to more than just drinks!

Chapter 6

Now back to the bar itself...

– Scene One –

PLACEMENT:

Avoid tables with friends. You might as well build a moat around yourself for all the action you'll get.

The ideal for you and, unfortunately, also the best for anyone else searching, is the middle seat of three empty bar stools. Next best, sit beside a friend, preferably one already with a b.f., with a vacant stool on your other side. And in either case, hope to avoid the cross-eyed man that sits next to you. "Actually, I was waiting to be picked up by someone much better looking" is a tough line to mouth.

Or simply stand, shoulders back, crotch forward, come-fuck-me smile on your face. Which makes this a good time to talk about...

Chapter 6

BODY LANGUAGE:

Most communication in a bar is nonverbal. A closed fist with the middle finger extended goes without interpretation in nearly every culture. Often without your knowing it, your other visible body parts also give signals, sometimes unintentional ones.

In a conversation, leaning a little forward is inviting, emphasizes sincerity, encourages acceptance. Within tongue distance of the ear is perfect, especially in a dark, noisy bar.

Your best lines will lose their punch if you don't deliver them while looking in the eyes of Mr. Target-of-the-night. Affect that detached or bored look on your own time, but never during the hunt.

Chapter 6

When talking with a prospect, do not look at the floor, out the window, at the clouds, into the crowd or at your cell phone. Eye contact. Eye contact. Eye contact.

After the eyes, the hands and arms are the strategic body-part communicators. Crossed arms generally say "keep your distance, unapproachable." (Texting while you're trolling sends the same message.) And keep your hands out of your pockets, unless you have truly mastered the "hooked thumb in the front pocket that simultaneously flexes your bicep and calls wanted attention to your growing hard-on" pose.

And speaking of hands, better to have the palms facing up (encourages communication, participation), and never have any finger pointing anywhere.

Chapter 6

Touching, of course, is the highest form of positive body language. An arm around a guy's shoulder or waist says it all. Then take his hand and head out the door. Taking control never felt better.

– Scene Two –

PREY SPOTTED, PICK-UP LINE NEEDED?:

Judge your prey. By his dress, by his drink, by his demeanor, and make a quick call for your opening line.

FIRST, this very important lesson in communications worth many times the price of this small book: You may not realize it but you **CAN** talk about almost anything with almost anybody!

THE SECRET: KEEP ASKING QUESTIONS!

Keep asking him questions about him and he will be fascinated and impressed with how interesting YOU are.

Chapter 6

In years past, there was a whole progression of questions to traverse as you gradually made your intentions knows. But in today's fast-paced age of thumbs-on-the-keyboard-communication, it's better to get right to the point with "Hi, you're cute/sexy/hot" and let nature take its course.

But if you need a template, after you get his name, go for the "what do you do?" and then try to fit your response to his answer.

For example:

If he answers, "I am a waiter," your response can be, "What are you serving up, tonight?"

If he says he is an accountant, do not ask for free tax advice but respond, "Busy time of year for you, isn't it?"—accountants always like to think they are terribly busy. Or, simply ask to see his assets.

Chapter 6

He is wearing glasses? Ask if he's really Clark Kent and is Superman under his clothes.

He is an architect? Ask him if he likes really BIG buildings or prefers smaller structures… with a naughty smile.

He is a lawyer? Resist the temptation to run. He may have a lot more than mumbo jumbo in his briefs.

If he is wearing his college letter sweater (very popular in the Northeast), a good opening is; "I was rush chairman… and I'm still recruiting."

Chapter 6

Then there are the spicy lines, good when you have your courage up (*three drink level*): "Nice ass. What time does it open?" "Do you sleep on your stomach? No? Can I?"

TECH AGE TRICKING AT THE BAR

"Call" boy now can be taken literally.

The electronic gurus were quick to realize the now ubiquitous cell phone can take the euphemistic "social networking" to new levels. An early standout – the iPhone with its great Grindr® app. A4A's Radar® is another.

Grindr®, (sounds almost sexually primitive), is the latest in high- tech tricking. Using GPS technology, Grindr® not only lets you know who is out there, what he looks like and what his stats are, but how close he is to you at that moment.

Chapter 6

Now the fun begins...

Without leaving your stool at the bar or appearing to take your eyes off the music videos, you can scan the room. You can cruise a park while sitting on a bench! Ditto a courtroom, the grocery or the beach. Or really get to know your neighbors. Find someone interesting? Just send him a text...or walk over!

Isn't technology great! And it's free!

A few rules and recommendations:

When you post your photo on Grindr®, it is prohibited to post a sexually-explicit one. Not that you would have considered doing that anyway. Who do they think they are dealing with? Really!

Chapter 6

The pic you post had better be a recent and accurate one. Grindr® is not designed for delayed tricking but for the here and now! With any success, you soon will be face-to-face with your contact.

Grindr® will tell you how many feet separate you from those listed. If the distance is near – the same bar, theatre or restaurant you are in, for example - a little subtlety is called for. No gawking! Better to case the room while doing the old neck or shoulder stretch.

If you like what you see, no pointing or hollering "Hi" across the room. On your part you don't want to risk a turn down in front of your friends. And there is the possibility he is with his significant, if temporary, "other."

Use the text-messaging feature to tell him where you are seated or standing and ask if he would like to meet. Then set your phone's call alert to vibrate, stick it in your pocket and hope for some sensation.

Chapter 6

PS: When choosing a Trick at a bar, go with (1) your intuitive gut or his lack of one (2) his build (3) his crotch (4) and/or his ass. Extra points for a seductive smile and definite bonus points for a real conversation.

Remember, every male in sight is your competition as well as your prey.

If you insist on being choosy, hang around 'til closing time when suddenly everyone looks good… but get out, hopefully with prey in hand, before the closing lights come up.

Chapter 7
ordering in

Chapter 7

ordering in
— how to get a tasty mouthful and not from the Chinese Carry-out

"Ordering in," or Cybersex, has definite upsides and downsides, not to be confused with tops and bottoms. Looking for a Trick online gives you the convenience of "working" at home with the fringe benefit that you can play with yourself (not impossible but a little more difficult in a bar) as you try to decide on your Trick for the night. Consider it "warming up."

Cyber searching has the advantage of giving some focus to your search. Old into young or young into mature? Silverdaddies.com is the matchmaker. You are a generalist? Sites like Manhunt or Adam4Adam or Gay.com are for you. Into bodies? bigmuscle.com takes the prize here.

Chapter 7

Into leather (reconleather.com), bears (bear411.com), kink (m4mkink.com) or jocks?(realjock.com). Whatever your fetish, you are covered. There is a site for everyone.

No matter what site you use, looking for a Trick in computer land does raise some cautions. Actually lots of them. But first let's focus on a big focus of your interest.

DOES SIZE MATTER? Duh...

The average male penis is 5.5 inches in length. Compare this to the average sex-site-sized dick which is 7 inches except on Manhunt where it is 7.5. The whole size thing is usually overrated and always overstated in AOL inches.

Chapter 7

Obviously a lot of guys think size matters. But there is a law of diminishing returns. Even if accurate at 8 or 9 or so, there are as many guys who would respond with "there's no way that thing is getting near me" as "yum." So while size may in fact matter to some, all would agree that much more important than what it is is what you do with it. Ninety minutes of energetic and creative performance is far more important than 9 inches.

For the international traveler, the following **Cock Converter** should be helpful.

Chapter 7

THE COCK CONVERTER

Inches	Centimeters	Quantitative Evaluator
5.5	13.97	Mathematical average
6	15.24	Marginally better
7	17.78	Time well spent
8	20.32	Now we're talking!
9	22.86	To beg for
10	25.4	To Die For or Run From!

Actual ruler included on last page of this book!

Dicks on a computer screen often look too small to be interesting, but don't despair. Start with the size shown and consider the possible coefficient of expansion. Also a larger screen helps.

Chapter 7

On the other hand, the cyber active learn that gay creativity and strategic camera placement can make objects appear much larger than they really are. The dick may be closer to the camera than you think and further magnified by your desires and testosterone level.

Have a cam on your computer? If a target does, too, you can verify some of his claims and maybe begin the foreplay before you meet. The downside: you can play too much and suddenly in a spurt of enthusiasm lose your motivation for Tricking. Mission aborted.

> *TIP*: As tempted as you might be to tear the previous page out, don't. Save yourself some time and a potential paper cut and just whip out that handy cell phone and take a picture of the page.

Chapter 7

DOES HONESTY MATTER?

If you are posting your profile on the internet, it's a highly-competitive world out there and some rule bending is expected — but never about health status!

Cyber honesty is relative at best. As you read profiles, add at least 10 years, subtract 2 dick inches, add 15 pounds and assume everyone is a bottom at heart.

Men who post pictures of their privates on a site that can be accessed by a couple million or more often "massage" the facts in their profile stuff. It's called mass marketing.

Chapter 7

But keep a guard up for real risks. For example, if you don't get suspicious when he lists his home address as the fresh produce section of Whole Foods, well, maybe you don't deserve to get laid.

Sometimes a creative approach will ferret out the truth. Remember there is a reported correlation between shoe size, ear size and dick size. Most guys post pics of the face, not their feet... check out their ears!

"How old are you?" is a question that often begs evasion. Better: "How long have you been on this site?" Assuming, (safely) he never has updated his profile, add his years on the site to his profile age. Reality becomes a little closer. Closer yet? Add 2 or 3 more years. But remember, before shaving too many years off your age, there is a definite demand for "silver daddies" out there as well.

Chapter 7

AGE, WEIGHT, HEIGHT, SIZE, POSITION — ALL FLUID!

Age: A safe rule is to add at least the same number of years you subtracted from your age when you posted your profile.

Weight: A safe rule is to add the same number of pounds you subtracted from your weight when you posted your profile.

Height: A safe rule is to subtract the number of inches you added to your height when you posted your profile.

Dick size: See above (re: height.)

Position: Assume everyone is a bottom and consider preferred position as flexible. He may think it is more masculine to be known as a top when it really depends on the company or the timing or the amount /quality of the "equipment" in play, not to mention alcohol intake!

Chapter 7

Smarts: Is his intelligence important to you? Likely you are not looking for the sharpest quill on the porcupine, tonight. Remember, this is a Trick. It's hard to give a quick IQ test. But if you really care about his brain size, hope for a correlation with that other important body part and aim for a Mensa!

Summary: Posting an honest recent pic is the best, and if you do, you have some license to fudge your physical stats a bit! But keep them within the realm of reasonableness. And If you have used a 1990's high school graduation picture as your current look-alike, don't be offended when you arrive at the scene and he explains you aren't what he ordered and closes the door.

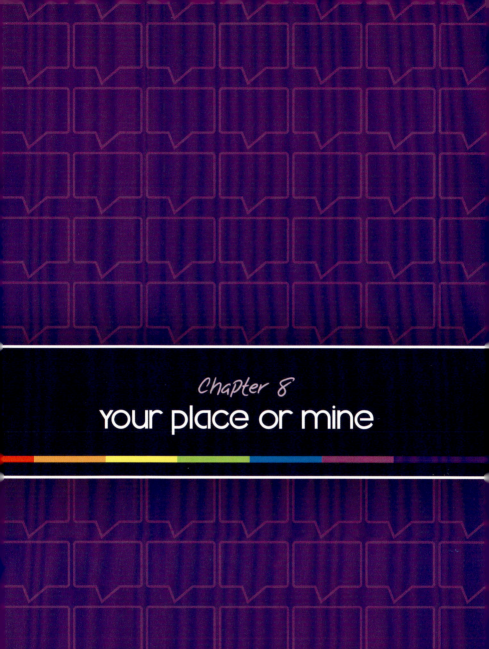

Chapter 8
your place or mine

Chapter 8

Your place or mine
— *who launders the cum towels?*

The location for the Tricking will be among the negotiations, online or in person.

Your Place:

Fresh flowers not necessary but fresh sheets are. Ditto fresh towels. But doing his laundry is not included.

Music: Sinatra, Madonna, Ella, Babs, Celine, Mariah, Whitney, Gaga or hard pounding (no pun) rock. Be ready for any (or all!) eventualities in mood. For the more visually astute, a "fuck film" playing in the background can provide both appropriate mood sounds and party ideas! A definite two-fer!

Bedside candles: nice touch unless poppers are being served.

Chapter 8

Share your toys. Accessories can be important. A nice display within easy reach can stimulate creativity. Encourage your guest to be creative... but you lead the way.

Trick tooth brush; Trick mouthwash; both front and center.

Always offer a shower before — and always offer to scrub his back. Ditto after.

Pets: Two (as in you and your Trick) is company. Three, if it is a four-legged third, is definitely a crowd. Keep your pets away. Your pet's barking, howling, or whimpering are not sounds to "rock the night away." It's enough that he may be intimidated by what you have under the sheets, but he is certain to be intimated by a Doberman in the doorway.

Chapter 8

His Place: (Definitely preferred so you can decide when it's over.)

> Be the good guest and be prepared: Bring your own condoms and lube, just to be on the safe side.
>
> Bring enthusiasm, energy, imagination and staying power. These will be far more appreciated than any "host gift." Remember, you're a Trick, not a dinner guest, although dessert does come to mind.
>
> Leave nothing but footprints. In the bright sunlight you will not look so pretty to your bleary-eyed host when you come back to pick up your cell phone.

Chapter 8

Have a clear plan on how to get home... and a few well thought-out reasons why, if that is an early necessity. Having a pet at home (real or imaginary), can come in handy as a great excuse to bolt.

Leave the lights, radio volume, rheostats, etc. where you find them. You are a guest... a participatory guest to be sure, but still a guest.

Do not fall into a relationship with his pets.

Remember he still will live here in the morning. Respect his neighbors. No running naked unless shades are closed; no door slamming or loud noise when leaving, especially if the hook up goes bad.

Chapter 8

Don't help yourself to anything: not his cologne, his razor, his cell phone and certainly not his toothbrush. A few exceptions: mouthwash, sure, to be shared. Poppers, if present, ditto. And of course, foil-wrapped accessories. In fact, feel free to ask!

COME CLEAN, at least physically. Do not bring uninvited, crawly guests.

Don't drink his last beer.

If you have to hide in the closet, be sure not to leave your shoes by the bed

Don't answer his telephone or his cell phone. It could be his mother, his WIFE, or **HIS BOYFRIEND —or yours!!**

If you are invited to stay over and he offers breakfast, be sure to ask first for a second helping of his special sausage.

Chapter 8

If the hookup is actually more date-like than Trick-like, (some cynics would argue a distinction with no difference), or you are a real house guest, take a gift, something very nice, tasteful and appropriate. (A copy of **Tips For Tricks** book immediately comes to mind!)

And if his lover walks in unexpectedly, say nothing (unless you speak ancient Sanskrit or some other unintelligible foreign language), get out quickly — dress in the street! Or... just move over and make room!

PS: A rule for host or guest. Don't fall asleep! And then there is the cardinal rule for all: NEVER CRY: Not out of excitement, not out of joy, not out of discovery, not out of embarrassment, not out of disappointment, fear or pain.

Chapter 9
no glove, no love and another helpful cliché

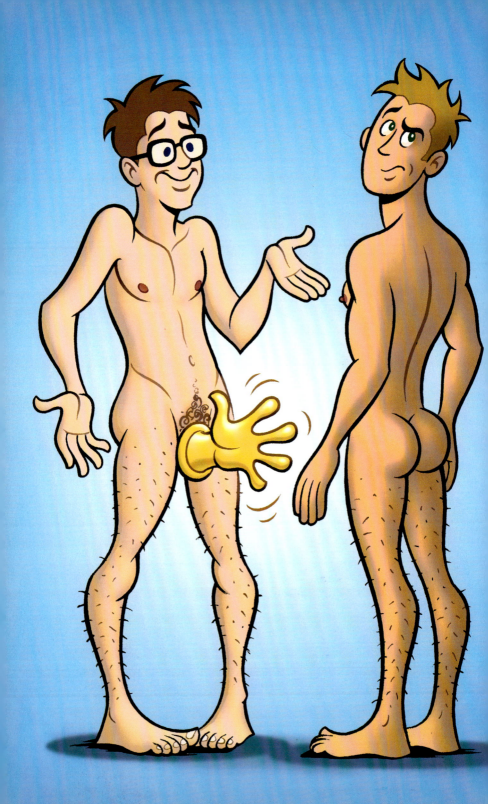

Chapter 9

"no glove, no love" and another helpful cliché
— two pithy points to remember

"No glove, no love" is a good cliché. Follow it. The good old days of the penicillin cure-all are long gone.

Rubbers are no fun? What's wrong with your creativity? Today, condoms come in all shapes and colors and sizes. Also there are ribbed and smooth, flavored and unflavored. There clearly is something to meet your preference. Experiment – see what you look and feel best in! And what HE looks and feels best in! Don't forget the fun of variety! And if you can wear a Magnum without the excess tip hanging down to the floor, your lucky partner will understand if you flaunt it.

Chapter 9

Practice makes perfect. It may be a bummer to "interrupt the moment" to put a condom on, but, done right, it can be a real turn on to erotically slide one on your partner's pole. And then, of course, it is his turn to have the fun of returning the favor.

Silence is golden. Chances are your hookup is not based on conversational ability. Good chances actually. Don't talk about politics, religion, boyfriends or strange perversions. Certainly don't talk about former Tricks! You will destroy the credibility of your pledge not to talk with anyone about this evening. (Soon to be broken, of course, with your friends) Actually the less said the better, honesty on health issues being the one big exception. If things go well there will be plenty of time to talk after... and maybe over coffee if things go very, very well.

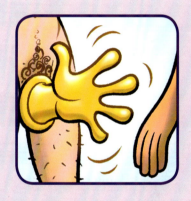

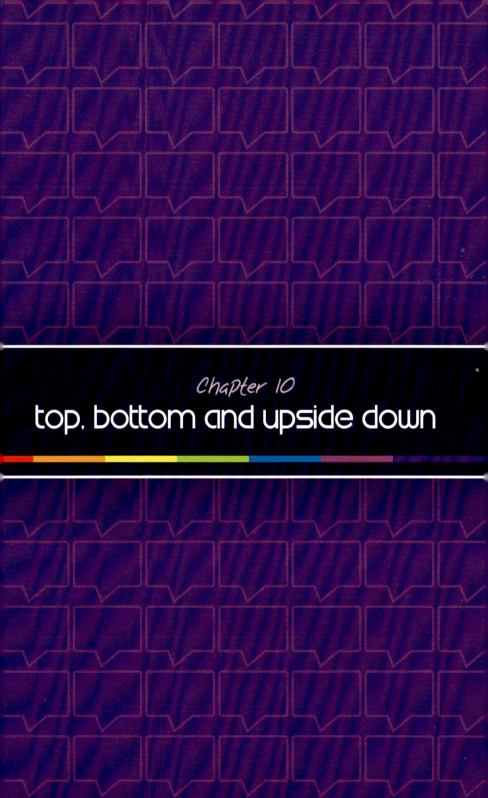

Chapter 10
top, bottom and upside down

Chapter 10

top, bottom and upside down
— is everyone REALLY a bottom?

"Top or bottom?" An even more serious negotiation than "your place or mine."

Timing is important. If you stake out a position (no pun intended) too firmly (again no pun intended, really!) and too early you might foreclose further negotiations later in the evening. In fact, the potential encounter might end even before it begins. On the other hand, if preferences (i.e., "what do you like to do" in the vernacular) aren't discussed ahead, the eventual hook up can be disappointing or even non-starting.

Chapter 10

If only the whole world were versatile. It is not! Of course your Trick may be a bit more versatile than he lets on and that can be fun to explore. A well-placed tongue has been known to open up new and unanticipated experiences

For some, the odds for ultimate satisfaction increase proportionally with the number of participants. For them, whereas 2 is always company, 3 is almost never a crowd and it's more like a sought-after experience! Math majors tell us the top/bottom usage ratio expands geometrically. If 1x1=69, then 1x1x1 must equal at least 69 squared or 4761. Unlimited openings and opportunities. Some guys like these good odds… and cash in.

Chapter 10

Now if the third (or fourth) is a boy friend, things can get dicey. A few tips:

In shorthand, "do the splits, don't cause them."

If you are "the third," always show equal attention to both partners. You will be attracted more to one than the other but you must play out and enjoy them both. You stand a much better chance of getting breakfast (including that special morning sausage) or being invited back.

If you are one of the BF's, follow your mother's advice and share and share alike. Remember, he's only a Trick! Sit back (or lay back) and enjoy the moment. Don't worry. BF will still be there tomorrow while the Trick likely will be long gone.

Chapter 11
bailing out

Chapter 11

bailing out
— just in case

Some hookups are just not meant to be, no matter how high the expectation. Know when to cut your losses. Let's be honest, not all have fairy tale endings (so to speak). Sometimes it just doesn't work out. You get to his place – or yours – and maybe you don't even make it to getting naked. He's too nice? Too raunchy? Stone faced? Stoned? Talks too much? Setting isn't right? Dust bunnies under the bed? Pets romping? Appearance of a surprise roommate you have Tricked with in the past? Or, maybe you have made it to the bedroom and his naked body reveals your x-ray vision was out of focus or he answers his cell phone and has a long conversation or he suddenly gets into kink you didn't know existed. Whatever. There are reasons for a turnoff and the best exit line is simply "You know, this just isn't working for me. Probably not for you either." That's non-judgmental and

Chapter 11

has a nice ring of finality. Also gives him some face-saving cover as you both get dressed.

An option: have a friend who is willing to call your cell phone 20 minutes into the hookup. This will give you an opportunity to use the excuse the call offers if the event is off to a bad start. You can always ignore the call (and enjoy the phone's vibration in your crotch) if all signals are go.

If the Trick isn't working, do the bailing out as early in the hook up as possible. Don't prolong the agony. An early decision to cut and run gives you (and him) the chance for greener pastures while the night is young. Don't waste time analyzing what just happened… spring back into action while your hormones are hyper.

However, the good news is most hookups DO work! Hence Chapters 12,13 and 14!

Chapter 12

the main event
— did someone say star power?

The main event. The hook up. No matter how you've met or where or what you've promised or lied about, it all leads to the main event. Let the fun begin. And that's exactly what the encounter should be. Fun!

Will you have a drink together first? Sure, maybe, maybe not. Will you make it past the living room before getting totally naked? Sure, maybe, maybe not. Will you gently undress or rip it off? Sure, maybe, maybe not. Start vertical, end horizontal, usually!!

On the furniture or on the floor? Either works just fine.

Chapter 12

There are no set rules, just enjoy all its many aspects:

touch lick kiss *taste* **enter** exit **prod** grope probe pinch tongue

Chapter 12

*In NO particular order

You get the idea. But keep the sex simple. Don't rush into any fancy stuff. You don't know what he likes, and he doesn't know what you like... and you have only a few hours to figure it out. So stick to the tried and true basics... at least at first!

Chapter 13
when to come

Chapter 13

when to come
— timing is everything!

Just as Vesuvius pretty much put an end to Pompeii, your eruptions likely will put an end to the hookup.

In the best of all worlds, the eruptions will occur simultaneously. When they do the event belongs in the Guinness Book of Records.

Go to any on-line "store" and you will find a variety of ointments to prevent premature ejaculation followed by ads for sensitizing potions to speed up getting off. And as noted above, alcohol and drugs can throw a wrinkle into any otherwise norm. This begs for a word of etiquette on proper winding down.

Chapter 13

If you get off first, the encounter isn't over. Pompeii isn't buried…although it may be flooded. Whether you are host or guest, there is an implicit "duty" in any Trick situation to lend a helping hand, a willing orifice or just plain dirty talk to give aid and comfort to your clearly still-horny partner. Opinions vary on how long this responsibility lasts….but clearly so long as he is getting closer and closer (verbal cues and twitching are a big help unless he is faking it). But after a while if his interest flags or his flag goes to half mast, it is reasonable to politely call it quits with words like "Sorry, I guess I've lost my erotic touch " or some such self- deprecating excuse for YOUR failure to get HIM off. It's only polite considering what he's done for YOU.

Chapter 13

And if you are the one whose performance has flagged, think of a good line like "You just have me turned on TOO much" or "I should have come earlier when I was ready but got selfish for more." Always end with "Damn!"

Chapter 14
when to go

Chapter 14

when to go
— breakfast is usually not included

With one or both eruptions now history, closed with the inevitable (1) "don't' move, I'll get you a towel" or (2) "want to take a shower?" it's time to pick up the foil-wrappings, bottle tops and dirty towels and draw the Trick session to a successful close.

Some small talk is fine as you are getting dressed. Be careful, though. Be sure to put on your underwear, not his. Exchange phone numbers? Sure, why not, although the odds are you'll never hear from him again. Still, it's polite to exchange and you've certainly already done significant exchanging with him already! End with the mandatory kiss at the door, not one last grope. It's just the right thing to do.

Chapter 15
after action

Chapter 15

after action
— maximizing the moment

Take a good hot bath and don't feel badly about yourself the next day. Giggle at your naughtiness. Call all your friends who are in relationships and tell them about your encounter. They will act outraged but actually will be pea-green with envy and they will enhance even your most vivid details of the story as they pass it along.

Give your Trick a call or text in a few days and tell him that you had a nice time… but make no plans to meet. This simple courtesy will allow you to greet each other without awkwardness when you bump into each other again. Remember "one-night" has a well-defined expiration date.

Chapter 16

into fisting?

You are far too advanced for this book!

the happy end*ing*

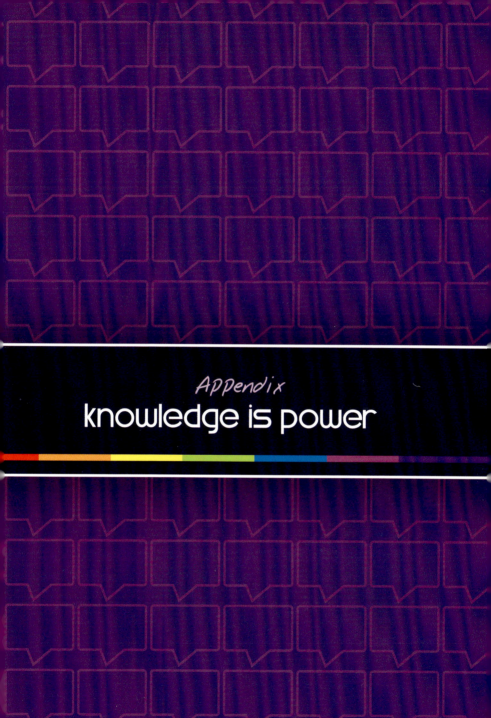

appendix

THINGS YOU WANT TO KNOW.

OUGHT TO KNOW.

NEED TO KNOW.

foreign tongues you will want to know
— *it's a big world out there!*

There are two types of foreign tongues. The kind that feel good and the kind that sound good. Here we focus on the latter. (Focus on the former on your own time.)

Since the gay world is multi-lingual, these phrases will be helpful:

How old are you? (legal ages vary!):

Spanish:	Cuantos años tienes?
French:	Quel age vous sont?
German:	Wie alt sind Sie?
Dutch:	Hoe oud sijn u?
Italian:	Como vecchio la sono?

I am a bottom!

Spanish: Soy pasivo

French: Je suis un fond

German: Ich bin ein boden

Dutch: Ik ben een bodom

Italian: Sono un fondo

I am a top!

Spanish: Soy activo

French: Je suis un sommet

German: Ich bin ein Oberteil

Dutch: Ik ben een top

Italian: Sono una cima

Are you HIV negative?

Spanish: Eres VIH negativo?

Dutch: Bent u HIV negatief?

German: Sind sie HIV-negativ?

French: Vous sont de negative de VI?

Italian: La sono l'HIV negativo?

do you have a condom?
— it can't be said enough!

This one is so important we want to be sure you have it in every language.

Bulgarian:	Mate condomu?
Czech:	Mate condomu?
Danish:	Har du et kondom?
Dutch:	Hebt u een condom?
Finnish:	Onko sinulla kondomin?
French:	Avez-vous unpreservatif?
German:	Haben sie ein kondom?
Hausa:	Kana da hular mabazuta?
Hungarian:	Biztosan van a kondom?
Italian:	Lei ha un preservativo?
Norweigan:	Har du et condom?
Polish:	Czy ma paprezerwatywie?

Portuguese:	Tem um preservativo?
Romanian:	Aveti un prezervativ?
Spanish (Euro):	Tiene usted un condom?
Spanish (Mexican):	Tiene usted un condom?
Spanish (Latin America):	Tiene usted un condom?
Serbian:	Lmate li koje?
Sweden:	Har du en kondom?
Turkish:	Sen bir pe ezervatif?

Touching, groping, eye contact and a friendly seductive smile all require no translation!

One cautionary international note: In some Arab countries, straight men walk down the street holding hands. **DO NOT BE MISLED**, that is just their custom. Unless you want to be **stoned to death**, which is not the same thing as being stoned, **forget it!**

hanky panky
— things you want to know!

This is especially valuable when visiting the Midwest, West, gay rodeos, and macho places everywhere else. These tell-tale kerchiefs or bandannas, sticking out from jean pockets, pack a wallop of information.

Color	Worn on Left	Worn on Right
Kelly Green	Trick for Rent	Looking for a Trick
Navy Blue	Top (Fucker)	Bottom (Fuckee)
Light Blue	Wants head	Gives Head
Black	Heavy SM Top	Heavy SM Bottom
Black/White *check*	Safe-Sex Top	Safe-Sex Bottom
Black/White *stripes*	Likes Black Bottoms	Likes Black Tops
Grey	Bondage Top	Bondage Bottom
Mustard	Has more than 8"	Wants more than 8"
Gold	2 looking for 1	1 looking for 2
Orange	Anything Anytime	Nothing Now

Color	Worn on Left	Worn on Right
Red	Fist Fucker	Fist Fuckee
Lavender	Into Drag Queens	Drag Queen
Lime Green	You buy dinner	He buys dinner
Hunter Green	Daddy	Daddy's Boy
Brown/White *stripes*	Likes Latino Bottoms	Likes Latino Tops
Brown Lace	Uncut	Likes Uncut
Brown Satin	Cut	Likes Cut
Beige	Rimmer	Rimee
Rust	Cowboy, wants to ride	Cowgirl, ride me!
Yellow	Into Water Sports	Thirsty
Coral	Suck my toes	Toe sucker
Red/Black Stripe	Furry Bear	Likes Furry Bears
Leopard	Has Tattoos	Into Tattoos
Tan	Smokes Cigars	Into Cigar Smoke
White	Jack Me Off	Will Do Us Both
Dark Olive	Military Top	Military Bottom

safety first
— because you need to know

This Tips for Tricks guide has been written in a fun and somewhat whimsical way. And life should in part be lived that way! But in any sexual encounter, no matter how much fun, there is a risk of sexually-transmitted diseases, a risk more serious today than ever. For good information about these risks and important steps to minimize them, check out these sites between visits to your favorite "ordering in" websites. It will be time well spent.

www.gmfa.org.uk/sex/

www.sfcityclinic.org/

http://psgaymenshealth.com

http://inspot.org

And then there are the drugs. This is a fast-changing environment. Today's designer drug is on tomorrow's drug clearance rack. Except for poppers, of course. They will last forever even if the rush does not. But remember, never with Viagra® or its wannabees.

But a serious tip about both alcohol and drugs: If you use, use carefully. Judgment is a terrible and dangerous thing to lose.

A Totally Helpful
glossary

a totally helpful glossary

Anal Beads: If you need to ask what they are, you may not be ready for them!

Butt Plug: Consider it training wheels.

Condoms: Definitely more a necessity than an accessory. We could expand on this subject or you can slip one on and expand it yourself.

Dildo: Devices to make porn stars money by licensing their names to un-humanly possible rubber penis replicas designed to bring psychological envy and physical frustration to all who buy.

Email: Preferred method used to exchange pictures of other guys' penises claiming them to be your own,

Feathers: To be used, not worn!

Google: Method used to find out how to use accessories you have never heard of but are curious about. Links to pics and diagrams are especially popular. A wonderful place, the web.

Handkerchiefs: Color-coded marketing tools; useful for spotting appropriate Trick targets in bars and clubs and grocery aisles; also used to identify what you consider too kinky, i.e., things you have not tried. Check "Hanky Panky" in the Things You Will Want to Know section of **TIPS for TRICKS**.

Incense: A bedroom mood enhancer helpful in masking popper and other sexual scents left over from previous encounters.

Jack-o-pump: Name says it all; user-friendly device to help your best-friend-right-hand assistant.

Kock rings: Here because we already had a "C" entry and too important to omit. A cock ring is used to make an erect penis harder and bigger, to keep it that way longer, and to delay and heighten orgasm. Pretty much says it all! Doubles as earrings for the really creative. *Caution: Unless you are turned on by the full-body search, don't wear the metal ones in airport security areas.*

Lube: A little dab will do 'ya and never has a little dab done so much for so many guys!

Ménage-a-troi or a-quad or a quint: Fancy for orgy... you pigs!

Manscape: (OK, so there are two "m's" get over it) Manscaping — that other "packaging." To shave down there or not? A shaving commercial says it all: "Makes your tree stand out in the forest!" Your lumberjack will love it.

Naughty: A great accessory-state-of-mind to bring to your hook ups. If you score right your Trick will bring the same accessory. Naughtier is definitely nicer.

"Oh Yeah", "Oh God", "Oh Fuck": The best verbal accessories... guaranteed to promote and encourage sustained Trick activity.

Pouch: Sometimes form over substance. Visually enticing, package-enhancing; new fashion accessory finding its way into pants, underwear and swim trunks. Now push-up-bra-wearing women have nothing on us!

Quickness: Not to be strived for. Nobody ever was invited back because he came too fast. In gay sex, stamina bests speed every time.

Rush: A popper-induced explosive - but short - euphoria. *Synonym: WOW. See also "Oh yeah, Oh God, Oh Fuck!"* But note, some guys lose their erection with "prolonged rushes" (maybe the ultimate oxymoron?). Use cautiously as an accessory... With your flame but not near one. And never with Viagra® or its copycats.

Spit: For the totally opportunistic but totally unprepared. Mother Nature watches over us!

Tupperware®: For holding lube, condoms, poppers, dildo, cum towel, whips, chains, slings and other accessories under the bed. Buy stain resistant.

Underwear: Going up the up-scale of sexiness, boxer to briefs to bikinis to bare buns. When making your decision consider pick-up-ability but also consider speed and ease of potential exit. Commando always wins.

Viagra®: Mother, or perhaps more appropriate, Grandmother Nature's little blue helper along with its followers, Cialis® and Levitra®.

Whore: Anyone who has had more Tricks than you.

X-rated: The seal of approval given to the very best accessories and to the best Tricks as well! A rating to strive for.

You: The best accessory of all for a successful hookup!

Zoo: What your hookup might become if three or more Tricks. See Orgy. (oops, no orgy entry... no matter, we all know what it means)

about the authors

Suffice it to say Bob and Tom have had more than adequate experience. They live and "do research" in South Florida... and elsewhere!

Special thanks to:

Glenn Hanson for the hot illustrations
C. Edwards for the creative design and layout

and

Indi Sukhra for her patience

To Do List:

	To Do	Done	Repeat	Forget
_____	☐	☐	☐	☐
_____	☐	☐	☐	☐
_____	☐	☐	☐	☐
_____	☐	☐	☐	☐
_____	☐	☐	☐	☐
_____	☐	☐	☐	☐
_____	☐	☐	☐	☐
_____	☐	☐	☐	☐
_____	☐	☐	☐	☐
_____	☐	☐	☐	☐
_____	☐	☐	☐	☐
_____	☐	☐	☐	☐
_____	☐	☐	☐	☐
_____	☐	☐	☐	☐
_____	☐	☐	☐	☐
_____	☐	☐	☐	☐
_____	☐	☐	☐	☐

(You might want to tear this page out for safe keeping!)

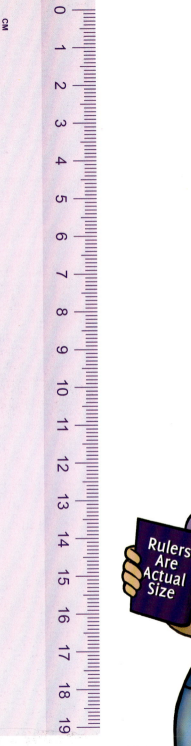